こんにちは私の名前はオ一月ラです。

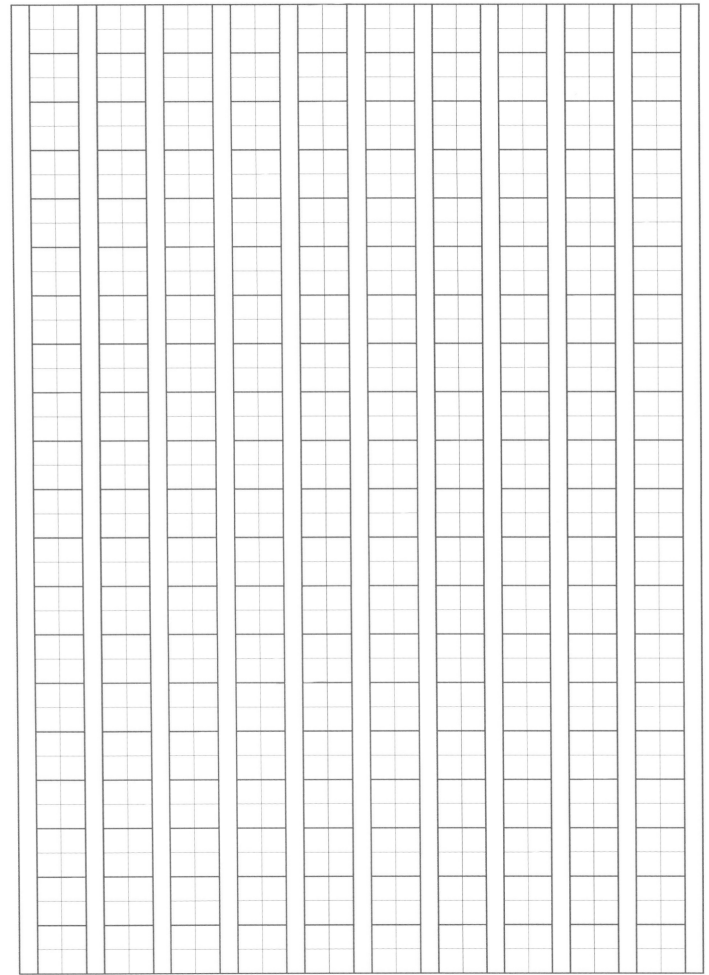

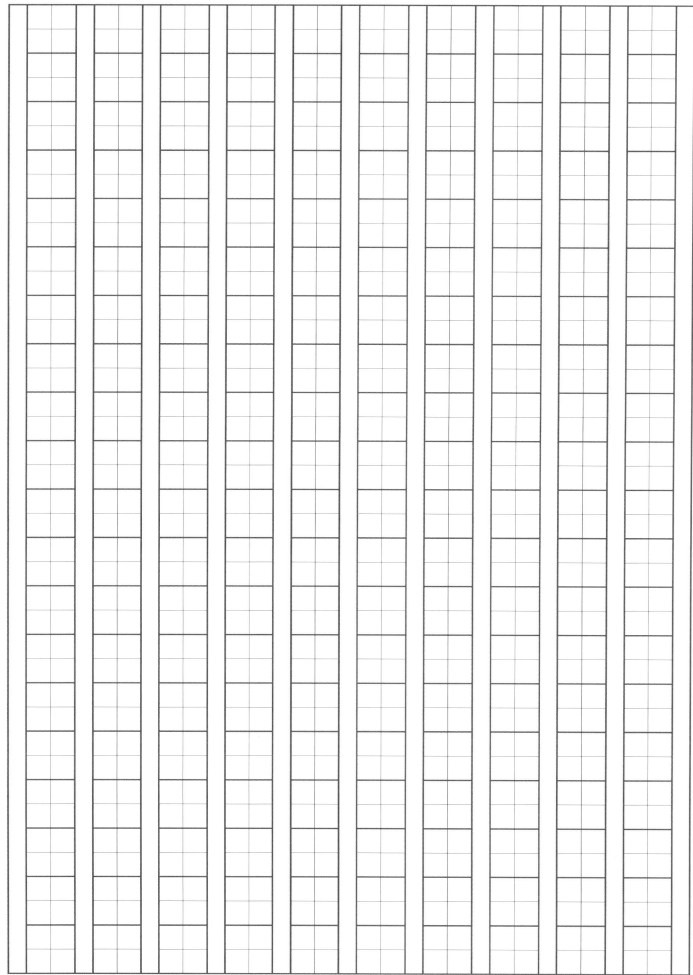

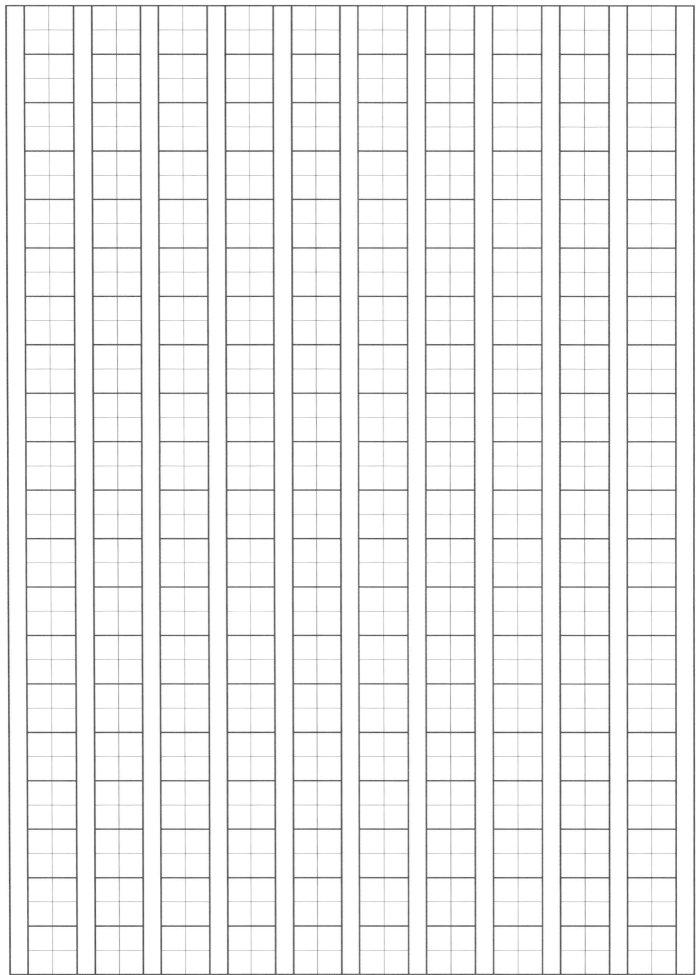

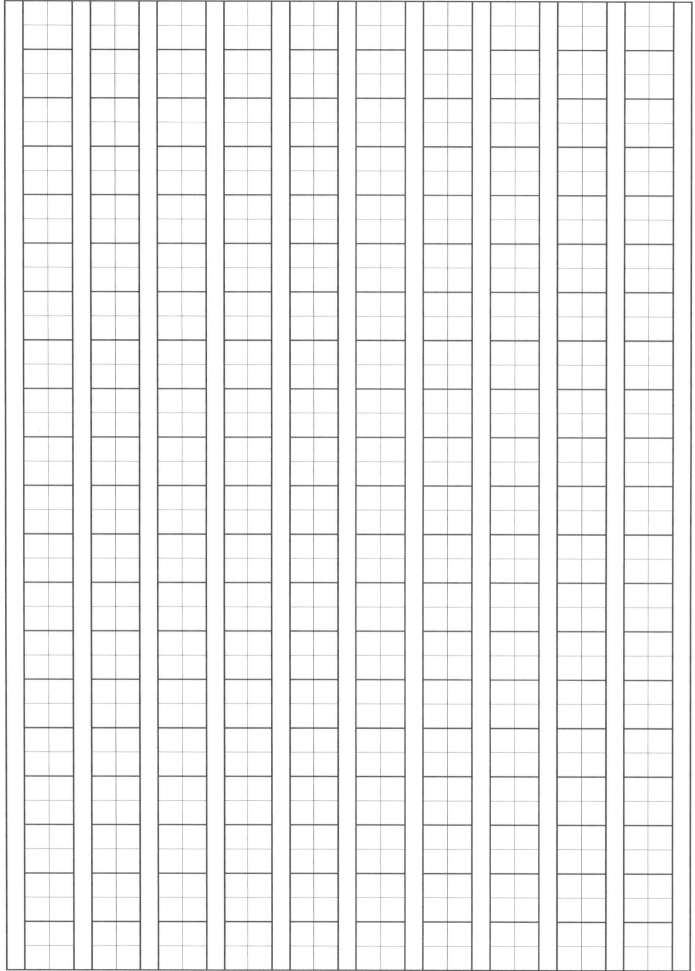

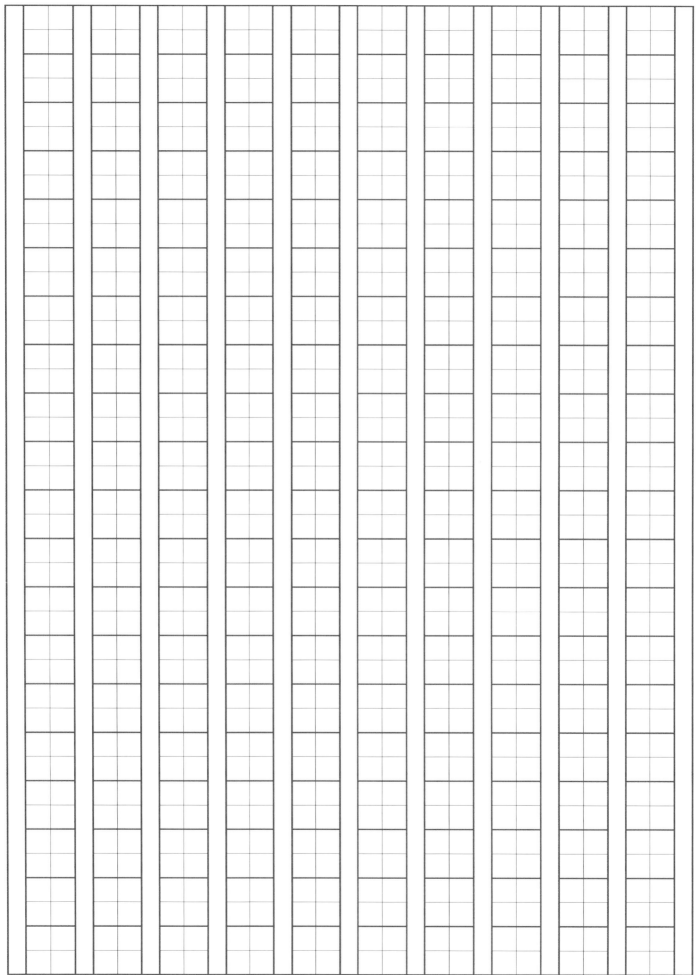

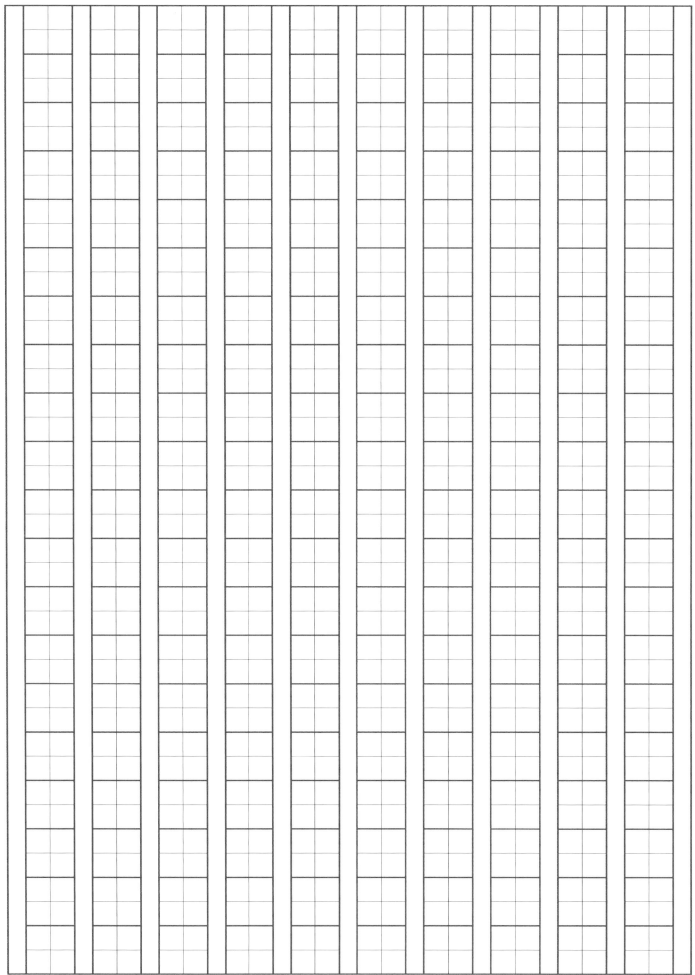

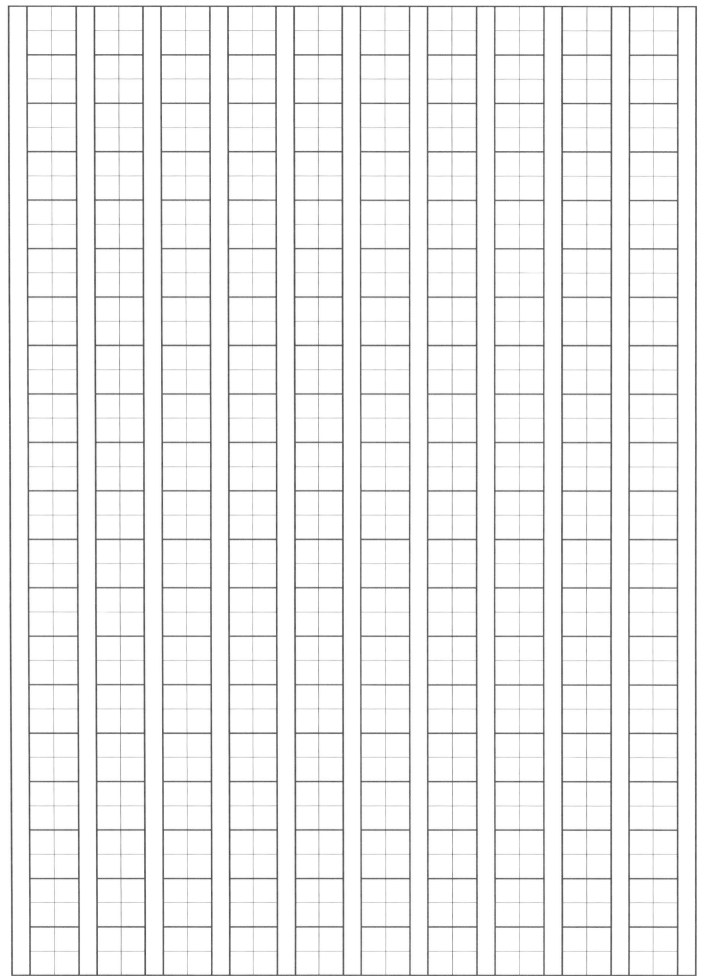

For more amazing journals and adult coloring books from Penelope Pewter, visit:
Amazon.com
CreateSpace.com
RWSquaredMedia.Wordpress.com

She Believed She Could
So She Did
Adult Coloring Book

The Be A Pineapple Adult
Coloring Book

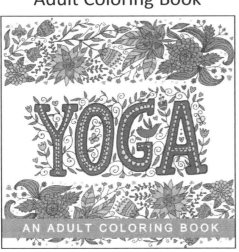

YOGA
An Adult Coloring Book

The Adult Coloring Book for
Coffee Lovers

Manufactured by Amazon.ca
Bolton, ON

21774609R00059